The Blueprint: A Guide to Answered Prayers

Published & Distributed by Live Life Production, LLC
541 10th St. NW, #2217
Atlanta, GA 30318
www.nadiathesuperstar.com
Copyright 2024 by Nadia D. Brown
All rights reserved. No part of this book may be reproduced in any form or by any electronic or mechanical means, including information storage or retrieval systems, without written permission from the publisher, except by a reviewer who may quote passages in a review."

TABLE OF CONTENTS

CHAPTERS

1. Acceptance - pg. 11
2. Prayers of Thanksgiving - pg. 16
3. Prayers of Repentance - pg. 22
4. Prayers of Mercy - pg. 27
5. Approaching The Throne of Grace - pg. 35
6. Blueprint at a Glance - pg. 42

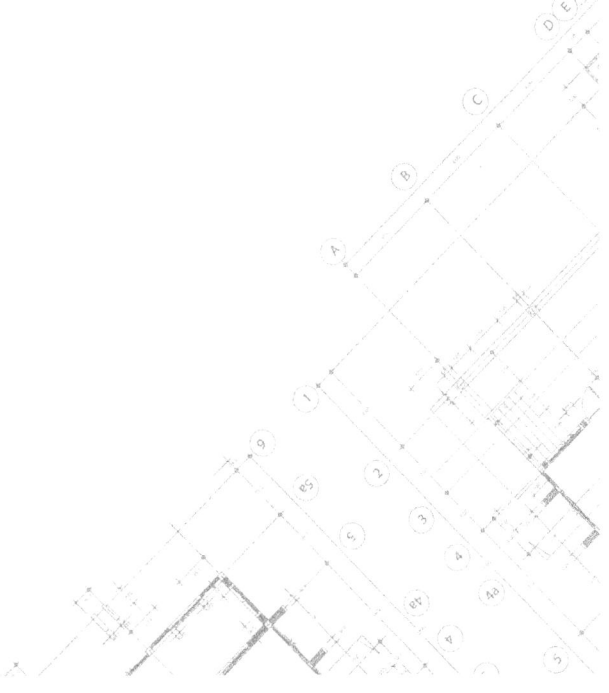

DEDICATION

I dedicate this book to God, the One who redeemed me and brought me back to Himself for His good works and pleasure. He is the God who spoke in Jeremiah 29:11-12 (AMP): *'For I know the plans and thoughts that I have for you, says the Lord, plans for peace and well-being and not for disaster, to give you a future and a hope. Then you will call on Me, and you will come and pray to Me, and I will hear [your voice and] I will listen to you.'*

I dedicate this book to Jesus Christ, the author and finisher of my faith (Hebrews 12:2), the One who left the ninety-nine to chase after me (Luke 15:4). He is the One who affirmed me as the righteousness of God (2 Corinthians 5:21) and who sits at the right hand of the Father, advocating for me (Romans 8:34).

I dedicate this book to my children Kimicion and Bryant, so they may always remember what it looks like to repair the breach in our bloodline. Know that after you have suffered for a little while, God Himself will come to restore you and make you what you ought to be! (1 Peter 5:10)

Look at the marvelous works of the Lord!"

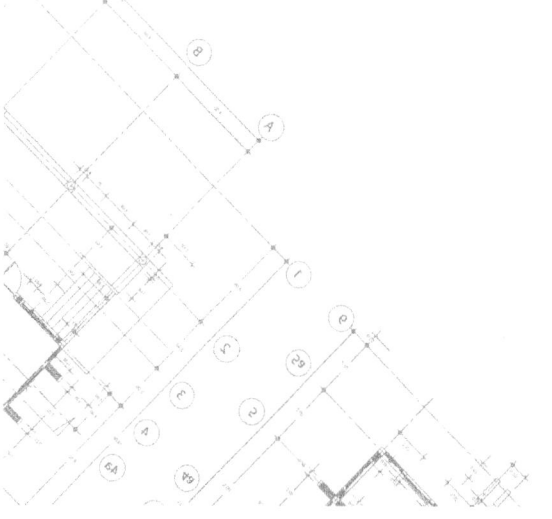
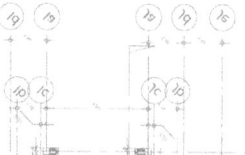

WHAT OTHERS ARE SAYING

"The Blueprint to Answered Prayers," a profound and divinely inspired formula, was shared with me by my sister Nadia. I am deeply grateful to her for passing this blueprint on to me. One day, when I faced a challenging situation, I shared it with Nadia. She texted me the steps of the blueprint and encouraged me to pray. Together, we stood in agreement, seeking God's wisdom and provision. As God is my witness, we saw His glory revealed that very same day. For every believer eager to elevate their prayer life and witness the tangible fruits of God's word in their lives, this Bible-based strategy is a must-read.

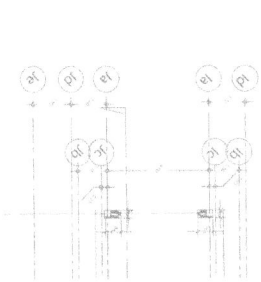
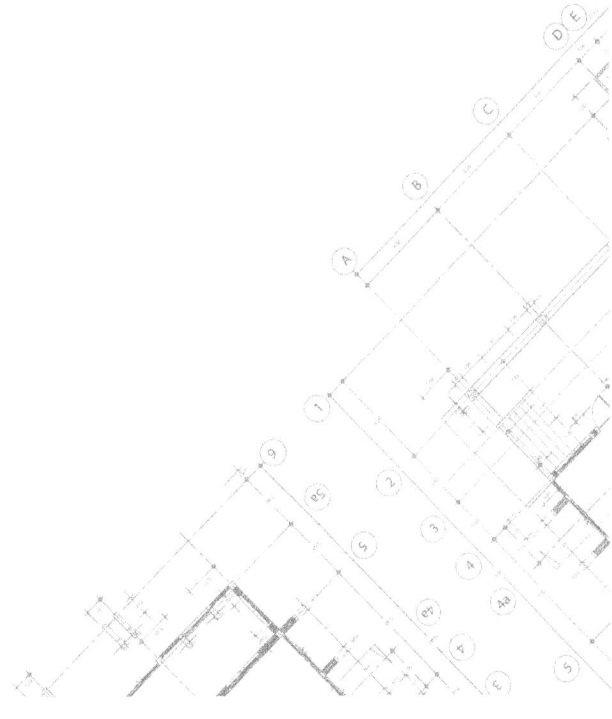

WHAT OTHERS ARE SAYING

On May 16, 2024, I reached out to Nadia, requesting her assistance in finding a new home. My move was scheduled for May 30th, but my applications were consistently rejected, leaving me with only two weeks to find a suitable place to live. Before our prayer session, Nadia reassured me that God would provide a solution and that I would have a home. We prayed according to the blueprint, giving thanks to God, confessing our sins, and seeking forgiveness and mercy. Nadia then cried out for God's favor and mercy before we approached the Throne of Grace. She placed a "Demand" on the application, requesting God's approval and favor for me to find a nice home before the end of the following week. Nadia encouraged me not to settle for less than I wanted and to trust in God's provision. She prayed on my behalf, asking for a nice home in a good neighborhood with enough space for my children.

A few days later, on May 22, 2024, I applied for a new home and was approved on May 24th. However, the rental company informed me that the home I had applied for was not yet ready for occupancy. This delay turned out to be a blessing in disguise, as I later discovered that the property I had initially considered settling for was not the ideal choice.

After waiting for 10 days for the rental company to prepare the home, another property became available that was even better than the first one. It had more space, was newer, and was priced the same. I was able to transfer my application from the first property to the new one and move in without any issues. All glory to God for answering our prayers and fulfilling our request.

INTRODUCTION

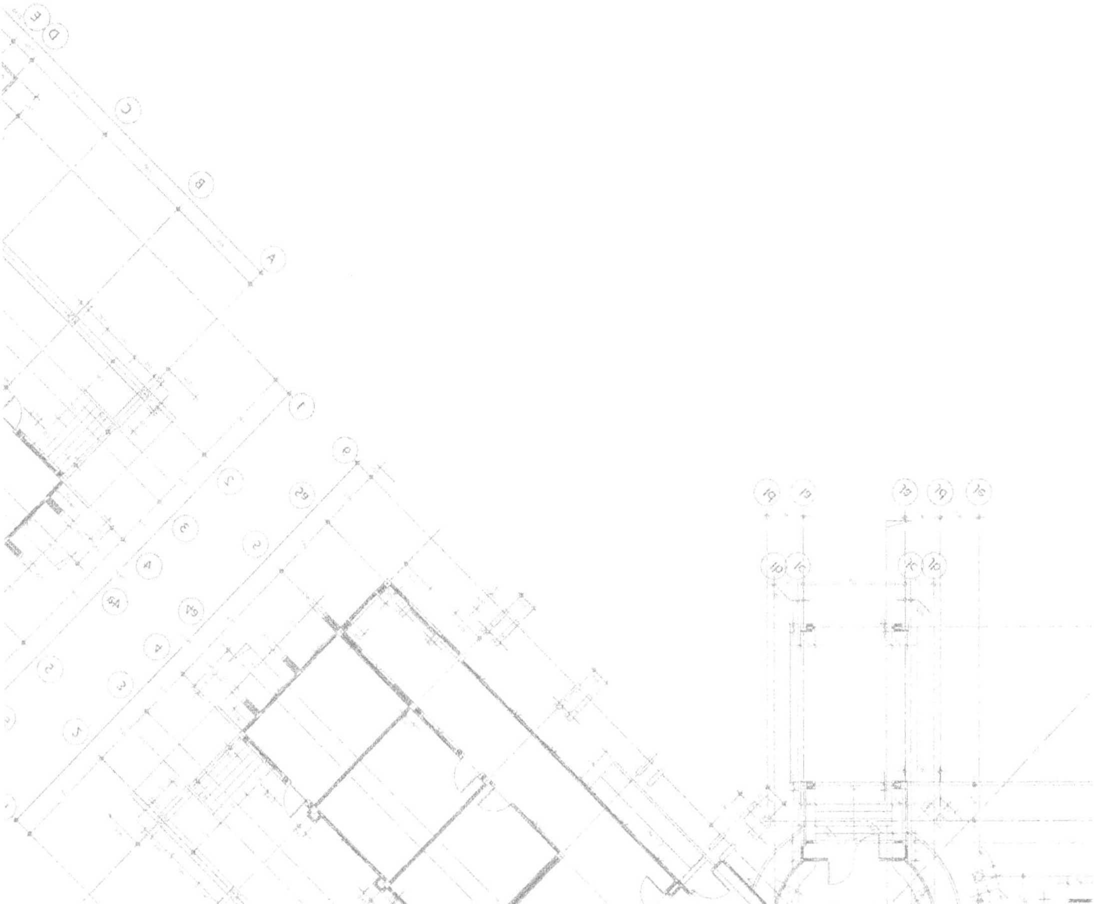

BLUE· PRINT

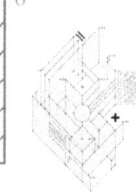

: something or someone resembling a blueprint (as in serving as a model or providing guidance)

: especially a detailed plan or program of action

You might be wondering, "Is there really a blueprint for prayer?" Given that we all have our own prayer language, style, and posture before God, you're right to think about the uniqueness of each person's prayer life. After all, God knows us intimately through our relationship with Him, which is fostered by reading His Word (the Holy Bible) and through prayer.

However, I want to challenge your perspective by suggesting that there is a blueprint for prayer. There is a way to approach God that not only reaches Him in Heaven but also moves Him to act on our behalf. These are the prayers that provoke God to incline His ear, not just to hear us but to answer us. I have personally experienced this divine move, which is what inspired me to write this book and share with millions of believers what I call "The Blueprint: A Guide to Answered Prayers."

Let me share a brief story about how I came up with this title. On February 22, 2024, I had a text exchange with my dear sister in Christ, Shontriska Jones. She asked me a question, and I responded with a new perspective, elaborating on it further. She then called me, and when I answered the phone, she said, *"Baby, you're the Blueprint."* I replied, *"Huh?"* She continued, *"You are the Blueprint. I just heard the Father say that about you. This wasn't even why I called, but the Father said you are the glue."* She explained, *"Think about it, sis, when you get something, you're going to build on it, give wisdom, lay out plans, and make it better."*

You may be wondering, What does this have to do with prayer? That same morning, God reminded me of a dream I had on January 28, 2024, where He gave me a business idea. When Shon spoke those words, it was as if the light bulb in my spirit turned on, and I instantly thought, *"This is the name for the business."* So, I wrote down *"The Blueprint"* as the potential name for the business. A few days later, I clearly heard: *"Write the book on prayer strategies."* I'm not even sure I processed what I heard; I knew what God was asking of me without him giving any additional details because of the space that I'd been in with Him lately, so I quickly agreed.

Why did I agree to this? I'm not a Pastor, I don't consider myself a prayer giant, Bible scholar, or anything of the sort. However, the more I thought about it, the more the idea of writing this book made sense in my spirit. Leading up to this point, I had noticed how quickly God was moving and answering my prayers, all by His grace and mercy. Holy Spirit began to highlight the strategy I was using as I prayed, and the power behind that strategy. My prayers were being answered swiftly—on the same day or by the petition date.

For those who may be unfamiliar, a petition date refers to a specific date, day, or time when we ask or request something from God. It's when we put a demand on God, giving Him no rest until He establishes what He promised. As Isaiah 62:6-7 (NKJV) says: *"I have set watchmen on your walls, O Jerusalem; They shall never hold their peace day or night. You who make mention of the LORD, do not keep silent, And give Him no rest till He establishes And till He makes Jerusalem a praise in the earth."*

As I contemplated writing this book, I began to realize that I'd grown exponentially in my relationship with God—especially in the area of prayer. God began to reveal that I'd experienced a spiritual growth spurt and my capacity, fervor, and authority had expanded. More than ever before, I was aligned with Holy Spirit and prayer and intercession had become an integral part of my days. I could feel the anointing of God shifting in my life. The authority and power in my prayers changed. It was a new realm, and God had done a new thing in me. This was no doing of my own; it is only by God's grace and mercy that He found me worthy to share this wisdom and mystery with others as Colossians 1:26 (AMP) says, *"the mystery which was hidden [from angels and mankind] for ages and generations, but has now been revealed to His saints (God's people)."*

I'm not saying this to boast or puff myself up, but I want to give you some context about how I arrived at this point—and it was all God. Of course, my obedience played a significant role, but God's mercies triumphed over every accusation the enemy brought before Him, questioning my qualification to write this book.

Romans 8:28-33 (NKJV) reminded me of how much I did, through God's justification and sanctification, qualify to pen this book. When God justified me—as if my past sins, failures, and mistakes never happened—that was the singular thing that would qualify me for everything God calls me to do.

He might be the firstborn among many brethren. Moreover, whom He predestined, these He also called; whom He called, these He also justified; and whom He justified, these He also glorified. What then shall we say to these things? If God is for us, who can be against us? He who did not spare His own Son, but delivered Him up for us all, how shall He not with Him also freely give us all things? Who shall bring a charge against God's elect? It is God who justifies."

As you navigate these pages, I hope that you will realize that God is not a respecter of person, and the same way He has redeemed me and allowed me to experience the power of prayer, the same is possible for you.

GOD WANTS US ALL TO MOVE IN THE DIMENSIONS OF PRAYER BY FAITH THAT YIELDS RESULTS

God's word declares according to Hebrews 4:16 (NKJV) *"Let us, therefore, come boldly to the throne of grace, that we may obtain mercy and find grace to help in time of need"*, and also according to His word in Philippians 4:6 (AMP) *"Do not be anxious or worried about anything, but in everything [every circumstance and situation] by prayer and petition with thanksgiving, continue to make your [specific] requests known to God"*.

You may be asking, *"How is this different from any other prayer book?"* I'm glad you asked! "The Blueprint: A Guide to Answered Prayer" is specifically for true Christ Believers. It's for those who have accepted Jesus as their Lord and Savior, repented, and have decided to turn away from their sinful nature and the cycles that once held them captive. It's for those who have undergone deliverance, placed themselves on the altar, and declared, *"I won't let go until You bless me, O Lord."*

This book is for those who have been halted in the spiritual realm by demonic forces preventing the blessings God has promised. It's for those who have prayed, and though the Lord has spoken, they still see no sign of the fulfillment of His promises—no sign of the prophetic words spoken over them, no sign of the dreams and visions God has given them.

The Blueprint, when executed with a clean heart, a renewed spirit, and pure motives before God, will change your life. It will restore your hope, trust, and faith in our Abba Father, who withholds no good thing from those who walk upright before Him. As it says in Mark 7:11 (NKJV): ***"If a son asks for bread from any father among you, will he give him a stone? Or if he asks for a fish, will he give him a serpent instead of a fish?"*** If our earthly fathers give good gifts, how much more will our Father in Heaven give good things to those who ask Him?

God is ready to show His Glory and Power through His children. As 2 Corinthians 1:20 (NLT) states: ***For all of God's promises have been fulfilled in Christ with a resounding "Yes!" And through Christ, our "Amen" (which means "Yes") ascends to God for his glory. God's Word is the only thing exalted higher than His name*** according to Psalm 138:2 (NKJV).

This is why it's vital to pray while fully armed with the armor of God, as described in Ephesians 6:10-18, utilizing the sword of the Spirit, which is the Word of God, also known as "The Holy Bible." Now that's how you stand on business, Kingdom Business that is!

So let the redeemed of the Lord go forth with confidence, knowing that when we pray according to God's Word and His promises, He hears us and answers according to our belief. I'm fully convinced that God will perform what He has promised, as stated in Romans 4:21 (NKJV):

The Blueprint: A Guide to Answered Prayer will allow you to experience a life of freedom, overflow, and restoration through revealed mysteries, as Jeremiah 33:3 (NKJV) says: ***Call to Me, and I will answer you, and show you great and mighty things, which you do not know.***

As you abide in God and His words abide in you, you will ask what you desire, and it will be done for you, according to John 15:7 (NKJV): ***"If you abide in Me, and My words abide in you, you will ask what you desire, and it shall be done for you."***

CHAPTER 1
ACCEPTANCE

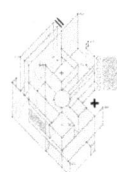

AC·CEPT·ANCE
: the action of consenting to receive or undertake something offered.

: the action or process of being received as adequate or suitable, typically to be admitted into a group.

The acceptance of Jesus Christ as our Lord and personal Savior is the first step in accessing God's blueprint to answered prayers. Again, as I mentioned earlier this is a prerequisite and won't work for those that don't believe in Jesus Christ. Let's be clear, this book is NOT some genie-in-the-bottle, get-rich-quick scheme. This book is a guide that will highlight our blind spots in prayer and expose how the enemy defeats us through our own ignorance, hence why God warned us in Isaiah 5:13 (NJKV) *"Therefore my people have gone into captivity, because they have no knowledge."*.

There is a spiritual ignorance in the body of Christ at large as it pertains to the kingdom of darkness and how the enemy fights us legally in the realm of the spirit. Those legal rights are given to him through covenants that were made with satan through bloodline iniquities, demonically influenced dreams, disobedience, idol worship of other gods and deities, inner vows, oaths, self-imposed word curses, sin, and unforgiveness, to name a few. Satan has been fighting us this way since the fall of mankind. It was the sin of Adam and Eve that breached the initial covenant of man which caused God to curse the very grounds in which we would stand.

Since the fall of man (Adam and Eve), we have been born into sin and shaped by iniquity.

'Iniquity' refers to moral corruption or wickedness.

As we mature in this fallen world, our character is influenced by the sinful environment around us.

WHEN INIQUITY IS IGNORED OR UNCHECKED, IT LEADS TO A CYCLE OF SIN THAT KEEPS US BOUND.

As Psalm 51:5 (NKJV) says, *'Behold, I was brought forth in iniquity, and in sin my mother conceived me.'* Psalm 11:3 (NKJV) says, *"If the foundations are destroyed, what can the righteous do?"* This verse reminds us that we can't build anything lasting on a broken or cracked foundation. From the beginning, we started life on a faulty and unstable foundation due to sin. Until we return to a right relationship with God by repairing the gap in that foundation, satan has a legal right to cause chaos in our lives. As believers, we must learn how to fight in the spiritual realm to destroy satan's plans and revoke his access to our lives. That's why restoring our covenant by accepting Jesus Christ as our Lord and personal savior is so important.

As the Word of God declares in Hebrews 12:24 (NLT): *'You have come to Jesus, the one who mediates the new covenant between God and people, and to the sprinkled blood, which speaks of forgiveness instead of crying out for vengeance like the blood of Abel.'*

God is raising up those who are unafraid to expose satan for the liar and thief he has always been. It's time to get your God-ordained, purpose-driven life back!

With that being said, there is a level of holiness and sanctification that God requires from us—an all-in commitment that declares: We are committed to seeking God's will and His purpose for our lives. We are committed to doing the inner work for ourselves and on behalf of our bloodline. We are committed to repairing the breach by renewing our covenant with God. We are committed to fulfilling the call of 2 Chronicles 7:14 (NKJV): *'If My people who are called by My name will humble themselves, and pray and seek My face, and turn from their wicked ways, then I will hear from heaven, and will forgive their sin and heal their land"*. Notice, I didn't say we are committed to being perfect because that's impossible. According to Romans 3:23-26, ESV:, *"for all have sinned and fall short of the glory of God, and are justified by his grace as a gift, through the redemption that is in Christ Jesus, whom God put forward as a propitiation by his blood, to be received by faith. This was to show God's righteousness because, in his divine forbearance, he had passed over former sins. It was to show his righteousness at the present time so that he might be just and the justifier of the one who has faith in Jesus."*

If you're ready to commit or recommit your life to Christ, simply confess the words below with sincerity. No one knows the heart of a person except the Father, as it says in Jeremiah 17:9-10 (NKJV): *'The heart is deceitful*

above all things, and desperately wicked; who can know it? I, the Lord, search the heart, I test the mind, even to give every man according to his ways, according to the fruit of his doings.'
God is calling you, so harden not your heart today."

Let's pray!

Dear Lord,

I stand here today as a sinner. Romans 5:8-9 (AMP) says, *"But God clearly shows and proves His own love for us, by the fact that while we were still sinners, Christ died for us. Therefore, since we have now been justified [declared free of the guilt of sin] by His blood, [how much more certain is it that] we will be saved from the wrath of God through Him."* I confess and repent of all the sins I have committed before You and against You.

Take a moment and begin to confess your sins to God. Be sensitive in this moment and allow the Holy Spirit to reveal things to you. Begin to call them aloud.

1 John 1:8-10 (NKJV) says, *"If we say that we have no sin, we deceive ourselves, and the truth is not in us. If we confess our sins, He is faithful and just to forgive us our sins and to cleanse us from all unrighteousness. If we say that we have not sinned, we make Him a liar, and His word is not in us."*

Therefore, I believe that Jesus Christ died on the cross for all my iniquities, sins, sicknesses, and transgressions. I confess with my mouth and believe in my heart that God has raised Him from the dead. I declare that Jesus is Lord over my life, and I de-throne every idol that I have erected to rule in my heart. I lay down every burden and cast all my cares at the feet of Jesus Christ. I declare under heaven that Jesus Christ has rule, reign, and dominion over my life. In Jesus Christ's holy name, AMEN!

Welcome to the Kingdom of God! As Heaven rejoices over your soul, I pray that you move forward with great confidence, knowing that you made the right decision and that your life will NEVER be the same. As you embark on this God-ordained journey, may the God who is able to do exceedingly and abundantly above all you can ask or think (Ephesians 3:20, NKJV) show

Himself mighty in your life.

I declare the grace of God over your life to stay the course, for this race is not given to the swift but to the one who endures to the end. May the power to endure be your portion as God begins to mold, prune, and shape you into what He fashioned you to be before the foundations of the earth. In Jesus Christ's name, Amen.

Psalms 139:13-16 (MSG)
Oh yes, you shaped me first inside, then out; you formed me in my mother's womb. I thank you, High God-you're breathtaking! Body and soul, I am marvelously made! I worship in adoration—what a creation! You know me inside and out, you know every bone in my body; You know exactly how I was made, bit by bit, how I was sculpted from nothing into something. Like an open book, you watched me grow from conception to birth; all the stages of my life were spread out before you.. The days of my life all prepared before I'd even lived one day.

CHAPTER 2
PRAYER OF THANKSGIVING

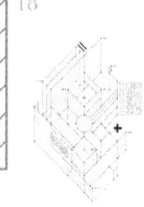 # THANKS·GIV·ING
: the expression of gratitude, especially to God.

Now that we have accepted Jesus Christ as our Lord and Savior, we move into the second step of the blueprint. There's nothing we could ever do to repay God for what He has done for us. What better way to acknowledge Him than with a heart of gratitude, expressed through prayers of thanksgiving?

 **OUR LIVES SHOULD ALWAYS REFLECT HOW GRATEFUL WE ARE.**

The Bible reminds us of this in Psalm 100:4 (NKJV): *"Enter into His gates with thanksgiving, And into His courts with praise. Be thankful to Him and bless His name."* The Message Version of this verse captures it even better: *"Enter with the password: 'Thank you!' Make yourselves at home, talking praise. Thank Him. Worship Him."*

God has given us the blueprint for entering His gates and His Holy presence—and it begins with a heart of thanksgiving.

Thanksgiving to God grants us access to come before Him to make our prayers and petitions known. It releases the peace that transcends all natural understanding, helps us to lay aside every burden, care, worry, and allows us to approach the Lord unashamed, vulnerable, and naked, as described in Philippians 4:6 (NKJV): *"Be anxious for nothing, but in everything by prayer and supplication, with thanksgiving, let your requests be made known to God; and the peace of God, which surpasses all understanding, will guard your hearts and minds through Christ Jesus."*

Thanksgiving to God is a way of recognizing and honoring Him for all He has done in our lives. Just as we enjoy being appreciated, God desires the same. Consider how we feel when friends, colleagues, or loved ones commend us for doing something good, honorable, or virtuous. It makes us feel appreciated and adored. It's no different with God; he receives appreciation and adoration from our thanksgiving.

There are simply not enough words to describe all He is or has been to us.

Now, let's take a moment to enter God's presence with the password "Thank you." Before we begin, find a quiet place where you can be still. Empty yourself of every care, silence the noise around you, and calm the traffic in your mind. Invite the Holy Spirit into this moment and allow Him to guide you during this time of thanksgiving to God.

Dear Heavenly Father,

Thank you!

Thank you!

Thank you!

Thank you!

Thank you for allowing me into your presence.

Thank you for inclining your ear to me.

Thank you for hearing my cry, prayers, and petitions.

Thank you for being a God that covers me.

Thank you for being such a loving and gracious Father.,

Thank you for being a father who withholds no good thing from his children.

Thank you for first loving me.

Thank you for loving me while I was yet still a sinner.

Thank you for Saving me.

Thank you for redeeming me back to you.

Thank you for sanctifying me.

Thank you for setting me free.

Thank you for loving me.

Thank you for justifying me.

Thank you for qualifying me.

Thank you for sending your only son that whosoever believes in Him shall not perish but have everlasting life.

Thank you for giving me this indescribable gift of life.

Thank you for the blood that was shed on the cross.

Thank you for being the lamb that was slain.

Thank you for being a Good Shepherd.

Thank you for leaving the ninety-nine to come and see about the one and that one was me.

Thank you for being the hills from which cometh my help, knowing that all of my help comes from you.

Thank you for being my advocate.

Thank you for being my anchor.

Thank you for being my bridge over troubled waters.

Thank you for being my battle axe.

Thank you for being my counsel of defense.

Thank you for being my great defender.

Thank you for being my deliverer.

Thank you for being my healer.

Thank you for being a just judge.

Thank you for being my mighty warrior.

Thank you for being my mind regulator.

Thank you for being my provider.

Thank you for being my restorer.

Thank you for being my strong tower,

Thank you for being my way over.

Thank you for being a heart-fixer.

Thank you for taking out my heart of stone and giving me a heart of flesh.

Thank you for delivering me out of snares set for me.

Thank you for giving me a way to escape.

Thank you, Lord.

Thank you, God.

Thank you, Emmanuel.

Thank you, Adonai.

Thank you, the Ancient of Days.

Thank you for being the Great I Aam.

Thank you for being the stone that the builders rejected.

Thank you for being the Chief Cornerstone.

Thank you for being a righteous God.

Thank you!

Thank you!

Thank you!

Thank you!

CHAPTER 3
PRAYERS OF REPENTANCE

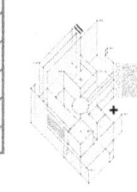

RE·PENT·ANCE
: to turn from sin and dedicate oneself to the amendment of one's life

: to feel regret or contrition

: to change one's mind

The third step of the blueprint is a very crucial one after one has accepted Jesus Christ as their Lord and Savior. This step centers on repentance, a key component of the Christian journey.

The Lord says in Isaiah 1:18 (NLT), *"Come now, let's settle this,' says the LORD."* The New King James Version puts it this way: *"Come now, let US reason together; though your sins are like scarlet, I will make them as white as snow; though they are red like crimson, I will make them as white as wool."*

Understanding that God desires to forgive us is vital to developing a heart of repentance. He wants us to lay it all out before Him and confess the things we have done that are detestable in His sight. Repentance is simply choosing to turn away from the morally corrupt nature that plagues mankind. The Bible identifies these sinful cravings as the desires of the flesh, which include, but are not limited to, the following, as listed in Galatians 5:19-21 (NKJV): *"sexual immorality, impurity, lustful pleasures, idolatry, sorcery, hostility, quarreling, jealousy, outbursts of anger, selfish ambition, dissension, division, envy, drunkenness, wild parties, and other sins like these."*

Repentance opens the door for God's mercies and brings freedom, delivering us from the guilt, shame, and regret that was birthed from the actions of our decision.

Repentance allows us, as children of God, to come before Him and confess any sin, whether known or unknown. This includes sins such as worshiping deities and other gods, engaging in idol worship—whether of the moon, stars, the universe, numbers, crystals, beads, or even people—and erecting evil altars to honor our deceased ancestors. It also covers the consequences of the actions of our parents, which we may now be paying for, as outlined in Exodus 20:3-5 (NLT):

"You must not have any other god but me. You must not make for yourself an idol of any kind or an image of anything in the heavens or on the earth or in the sea. You must not bow down to them or worship them, for I, the Lord your God, am a jealous God who will not tolerate your affection for any other gods. I lay the sins of the parents upon their children; the entire family is affected—even children in the third and fourth generations of those who reject me."

REPENTANCE CREATES A SPACE OF HONESTY WITH BOTH GOD AND OURSELVES.

It's a sacred space where we can come before God, naked and unashamed, knowing that nothing surprises Him. After all, God placed His promises about us in the finished work of Jesus Christ.

As Psalms 139:1-5 (TPT) says:

"Lord, you know everything there is to know about me. You perceive every movement of my heart and soul, and you understand my every thought before it even enters my mind. You are so intimately aware of me, Lord. You read my heart like an open book, and you know all the words I'm about to speak before I even start a sentence! You know every step I will take before my journey even begins."

REPENTING IS A SPACE OF EMPTYING AND DUMPING ALL OF THE "SHOULDA," "COULDA," AND "WOULDA" WOES OF LIFE.

There is great provision in repentance, as it is the first step toward living a life of freedom, as stated in Acts 3:19 (NKJV): *"Repent therefore and be converted, that your sins may be blotted out, so that times of refreshing may come from the presence of the Lord."*

Refreshing means to be made new. Repentance allows you to shed the stains of your old self and step into the newness of life in Christ. Repenting before God cleanses our hands and purifies our hearts, allowing us to ascend to the hills of the Lord (Psalms 24:3-4). The enemy can no longer torment you with past failures, guilt, mistakes, or shame, because you have acknowledged them before God.

We serve a God who is a just judge and who is faithful to forgive us, as stated in 1 John 1:8-10 (NKJV): *"If we say that we have no sin, we deceive ourselves, and the truth is not in us. If we confess our sins, He is faithful and just to forgive us our sins and to cleanse us from all unrighteousness. If we say that we have not sinned, we make Him a liar, and His word is not in us."*

Imagine for a moment that we are given a seat in the courts of Heaven, cases of repentance would go something like this:

Satan vs. the Repented Believer

Prosecutor: *Your Honor, the prosecutor [also known as the accuser of the brethren and a liar] would like to read the charges of the defendant before the court.*

Counsel of Defense [also known as Jesus]: *Objection, Your Honor. The defendant has been exonerated of all charges being brought before the courts of heaven. The blood of Jesus served as evidence on behalf of the defendant, which makes the evidence from the accuser inadmissible in this court.*

The Just Judge [also known as God]: *Sustained. This case is dismissed, and the defendant is free to go on the grounds of inadmissible evidence due to the Blood of Jesus.*

This inadmissible evidence causes Satan to relinquish his power and drop the charges against us, as declared in Romans 8:1 (TPT): *"So now the case is closed. There remains no accusing voice of condemnation against those who have joined their lives in unison with Jesus, the Anointed One."* This is why the Bible tells us in Matthew 5:25 (NKJV) **to QUICKLY agree with the adversary, before he drags us off to court;** so we should confess the sin, repent, and turn away from it.

I'll leave you with this passage of scripture written by King David who knew all too well about the power of repentance and the restoration that follows. He who has an ear to hear, let him hear:

Psalms 32:1-6 (NLT):
"Oh, what joy for those whose disobedience is forgiven, whose sin is put out of sight! Yes, what joy for those whose record the Lord has cleared of guilt, whose lives are lived in complete honesty! When I refused to confess my sin, my body wasted away, and I groaned all day long. Day and night your hand of discipline was heavy on me. My strength evaporated like water in the summer heat. Finally, I confessed all my sins to you and stopped trying to hide my guilt. I said to myself, 'I will confess my rebellion to the Lord.' And you forgave me! All my guilt is gone. Therefore, let all the godly pray to you while there is still time, that they may not drown in the floodwaters of judgment."

Take a moment right now, go before the Lord, and repent. Allow Holy Spirit to lead you during this process. Don't hold anything back, for the Lord already knows everything we've done. He's just waiting for us to *CONFESS it*.

CHAPTER 4

PRAYERS OF MERCY

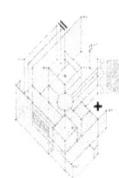

MER·CY

: a blessing that is an act of divine favor or compassion

: compassionate or kindly forbearance shown toward an offender, an enemy, or other person in one's power; compassion, pity, or benevolence

We've now come to the point in prayer where we have reached the door of MERCY. This door is opened to us through true repentance, which is the act of turning away from and having a change of heart and mind. It is God's great desire to show forth His mercy toward us, hence why He sent our savior, Jesus Christ.

According to 1 Peter 1:3 (NLT), *"All praise to God, the Father of our Lord Jesus Christ. It is by his great MERCY that we have been born again because God raised Jesus Christ from the dead. Now we live with great expectation."*

The expectation is knowing that we have been placed back in right standing with God through our Savior, Jesus Christ. According to Ephesians 2:1-7 (NLT), *"Once you were dead because of your disobedience and your many sins. You used to live in sin, just like the rest of the world, obeying the devil—the commander of the powers in the unseen world. He is the spirit at work in the hearts of those who refuse to obey God. All of us used to live that way, following the passionate desires and inclinations of our sinful nature. By our very nature, we were subject to God's anger, just like everyone else. But God is so rich in MERCY, and he loved us so much, that even though we were dead because of our sins, he gave us life when he raised Christ from the dead. (It is only by God's grace that you have been saved!) For he raised us from the dead along with Christ and seated us with him in the heavenly realms because we are united with Christ Jesus. So, God can point to us in all future ages as examples of the incredible wealth of his grace and kindness toward us, as shown in all he has done for us who are united with Christ Jesus."*

God is so genius and mindful of us that he gave us a literal "Blueprint" to experience and live out our God-ordained, purpose-filled life of authority, fulfillment, joy, love, peace, and much more.

As it is written according to Psalms 8:4-6 (NKJV), *"What is man that You are mindful of him, And the son of man that You visit him? For You have made him a little lower than the angels, And You have crowned him with glory and honor. You have made him to have dominion over the works of Your hands; You have put all things under his feet."*

I've come to realize that God is truly the Creator of everything. When He created humanity, He knew we would fall, that we would sin, and that the enemy would battle against us and prevail for as long as we would be unaware of his tactics. He knew all of this—and more—and still decided that we were worth redemption.

There's nothing that God doesn't know, which is the reason why from the foundations of the earth, He appointed Himself to be our human savior known as Jesus Christ. A savior that is *RICH in MERCY.* God has allowed us to trace his merciful nature to Adam and Eve. One may ask, "How did He show them mercy when He kicked them out of the Garden of Eden and cursed them both?" I'd like to challenge that thought by stating that He was *MERCIFUL* in that He could've killed them both which would've ended mankind's existence on earth, but because of the *LOVE and MERCY* He has for HIS creation and the earth at large, HE permitted man to live to fulfill his intended purpose.

We've come to a point in prayer where it is *ONLY* the *MERCIES* of God that can overturn, overrule, and overthrow the accusations and judgments of satan. However, many of us have been conditioned to see mercy as just a casual or overlooked gesture, something we take for granted, much like we do with grace.

WE OFTEN FAIL TO UNDERSTAND THAT IT IS GOD'S MERCY THAT PREVENTS THE CONSEQUENCES OF OUR SINS FROM DESTROYING US

Even though, truth be told, we are guilty and deserve the punishment prescribed by the law, which is why the Bible tells us in Matthew 5:25-26 to agree with our adversary quickly!

Let's be honest, we have done *ALL* the things that the enemy consistently brings before God as it pertains to our sins individually, and collectively through the iniquitous patterns of our bloodline and mankind overall. We have moved in disobedience; we have committed disgusting acts toward God; and we have blatantly disobeyed His instructions and Word. In other words, *WE HAVE PLAYED IN GOD'S FACE* and have sinned openly before God far too long and it's time we repent and cry out for His everlasting *MERCY* because our best deeds, works, and service unto God are as filthy rags before him as stated in Isaiah 64:6-7: ***"We are all infected and impure with sin. When we display our righteous deeds, they are nothing but filthy rags. Like autumn leaves, we wither and fall, and our sins sweep us away like the wind. Yet no one calls on your name or pleads with you for MERCY. Therefore, you have turned away from us and turned us over to our sins."***

As we begin to call upon our counsel of defense, Jesus Christ, the one who advocates for us at the right hand of the Father, the one who pleads our case, the one who paid the price for our sins with His own blood and life, and the one who presents us faultless and not guilty before the Just Judge and merciful God— remember it is through our confession that we receive mercies, which are made new to us every morning.

According to Lamentations, 3:21-24 (NKJV), ***"This I recall to my mind; therefore I have hope. Through the Lord's mercies, we are not consumed, Because His compassions fail not. They are new every morning; Great is Your faithfulness. 'The Lord is my portion,' says my soul, 'Therefore I hope in Him!'"***

I'd like to remind you that God's mercies triumph over judgment—meaning judgment cannot stand against the mercies of God, which grant us victory. As I walked out this Blueprint to answered prayers, Holy Spirit revealed that there is provision in obedience to God, provision in repentance, and provision when we cry out for God's mercy in our lives and situations.

Let's take time to enter God's presence as we pray and cry out for mercy. Please allow this prayer to serve as a guide on how to access God's compassion through prayer.

God, thank you for the love and kindness you've shown me as I've entered your gates with the password 'Thank You', as I have accepted you to be my Lord and personal savior; as I have confessed my sins before you and sins on behalf of my bloodline. I know that you have forgiven me and have chosen not to remember the sin anymore and for that, I say THANK YOU. Thank you for your mercy that has been made new to me every morning, thank you Lord that according to your word in James 2:13 (NKJV), *"for judgment is without mercy to the one who has shown no mercy." Mercy triumphs over judgment.* I know it is your mercy that shuts the mouth of the enemy. It is your mercy that destroys yokes and reconciles families. It is your mercy that allows me to find rest in you. It is your mercy that allows me to experience your peace. It is your mercy that allows doors to be open unto me that were once closed. It is your mercy that fast tracks my life to the place that I should be. It is your mercy that causes people to extend favor to me. It is your mercy that causes all grace to abound toward me. It is your mercy that allows me to gain access to your throne of Grace. It is your mercy that allows me to receive your revelation. It is your mercy that you choose to uphold me with your righteous right hand. It is your mercy that allows me to find safety in your counsel and it is because of your great mercy that you choose to save a wretch like me. For that, I say Thank You and have Mercy on me oh Lord, in Jesus Christ's name I pray Amen!

Isaiah 51:1-17 (NKJV)
Have mercy upon me, O God,
According to Your lovingkindness;
According to the multitude of Your tender mercies,
Blot out my transgressions.
Wash me thoroughly from my iniquity,
And cleanse me from my sin.
For I acknowledge my transgressions,
And my sin is always before me.
Against You, You only, have I sinned,
And done this evil in Your sight—
That You may be found just when You speak,
And blameless when You judge.
Behold, I was brought forth in iniquity,
And in sin, my mother conceived me.
Behold, You desire truth in the inward parts,
And in the hidden part, You will make me to know wisdom.
Purge me with hyssop, and I shall be clean;
Wash me, and I shall be whiter than snow.
Make me hear joy and gladness,
That the bones You have broken may rejoice.

Hide Your face from my sins,
And blot out all my iniquities.
Create in me a clean heart, O God,
And renew a steadfast spirit within me.
Do not cast me away from Your presence,
And do not take Your Holy Spirit from me.
Restore to me the joy of Your salvation,
And uphold me by Your generous Spirit.
Then I will teach transgressors Your ways,
And sinners shall be converted to You.
Deliver me from the guilt of bloodshed, O God,
The God of my salvation,
And my tongue shall sing aloud of Your righteousness.
O Lord, open my lips,
And my mouth shall show forth Your praise.
For You do not desire sacrifice, or else I would give it;
You do not delight in burnt offering.
The sacrifices of God are a broken spirit,
A broken and contrite heart—
These, O God, You will not despise.

WHAT OTHERS ARE SAYING

On May 13th, I received an email from my son's counselor informing me that he wasn't cleared to graduate due to a failing grade in Physics. His teacher had already been difficult to deal with—that's a story for another time—but she had told him that he could pass the class by completing a lab and passing his final and a makeup test. He did both, yet she still tried to fail him.

Fast forward to that Friday: When my son went to complete the lab, the teacher refused to help him. She even stopped the assistant teacher from offering support and bluntly told him he wasn't going to pass the class. This would mean summer school, which would prevent him from graduating on time and walking with his class. My son was so upset that he called me in tears, venting about the unfairness of the situation. I told him to calm down, stay respectful, and not engage in an argument.

It became clear that the teacher was determined for him to fail—she had even entered a failing grade in the system. And the deadline for grades was just two days away on May 15th.

After that incident, I used the moment to teach my son an important lesson. I reminded him that his own procrastination and inconsistent attendance gave her the ammunition she needed. I had already warned him earlier in the year that the enemy wanted to block his graduation and bring shame. The Holy Spirit had also revealed to him months ago that the devil wanted him to drop out, just like his dad. But I reassured him that the devil can't steal what God has marked as His.

The next day, I received another email from the counselor saying the teacher refused to let him complete the lab due to his attendance, but he was still expected to come to class until May 24th to "try" to pass, even though the grades were due by May 15th. Something wasn't adding up.

That morning, I prayed, following the principles laid out in *The Blueprint*. I gave thanks, repented, cried out for mercy, and asked God for guidance. Should I get involved, or let my son handle it? The Lord told me to step back.

I told my son to pray for vindication, to repent for the part he played, and to ask God for mercy. He said, "I did, Mom. I prayed hard this morning." I suggested he talk to the department head.

It wasn't easy, but I had to trust God.

Not even two hours later, my son called me. His former 6th grade English teacher, who was now an administrator, had called him into her office. She looked into the situation and discovered that on the day the lab was due, he wasn't skipping class as the teacher claimed—he had an early dismissal! She immediately sent an email to the head of the science department and assured me she'd investigate further.

By the end of the day, the assistant principal FaceTimed me to say he had spoken with the physics teacher to get more information. By the next morning, he was allowed to complete the lab that she had initially refused him. He passed the lab, passed the course, and was cleared for graduation!

That same day, I joined my prayer call, and one of my sisters in Christ began praying specifically against demonic delays that would block our children from graduating. She didn't know what I had been going through, but God did. The Holy Spirit had sent reinforcements!

In Jesus' name, there will be no more delays or hindrances. Our children will finish on time. And praise God, my son did just that!

CHAPTER 5

APPROACHING THE THRONE OF GRACE

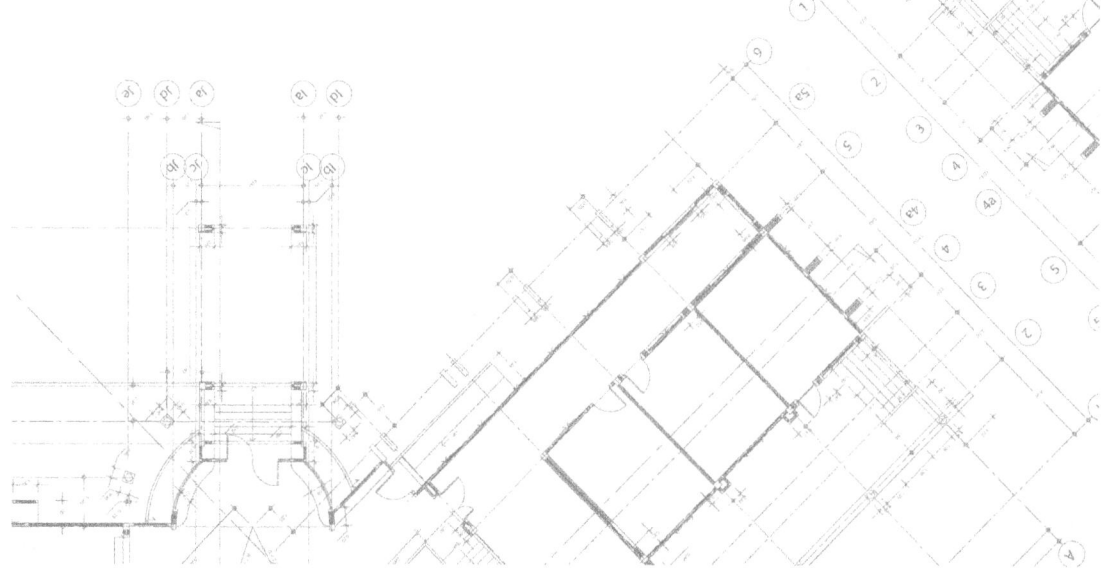

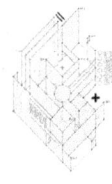

GRACE

: unmerited divine assistance given to humans for their regeneration or sanctification

: a virtue coming from God

: a state of sanctification enjoyed through divine assistance

: APPROVAL, FAVOR
archaic: MERCY, PARDON

: a special favor: PRIVILEGE

: disposition to or an act or instance of kindness, courtesy, or clemency

: a temporary exemption: REPRIEVE

The biblical usage of grace is:

: that which affords joy, pleasure, delight, sweetness, charm, loveliness: grace of speech

: goodwill, loving-kindness, favor.

: of the merciful kindness by which God, exerting his holy influence upon souls, turns them to Christ, keeps, strengthens, increases them in Christian faith, knowledge, affection, and kindles them to the exercise of the Christian virtues.

: the spiritual condition of one governed by the power of divine grace: the token or proof of grace, benefit - a gift of grace.

: thanks, (for benefits, services, favors), recompense, reward

Now that our hearts have been purified and we have clean hands, we have been given clearance to go before the Lord, according to Psalms 24:3-4 (NKJV). This is also not a time to be anxious for anything. Instead, make your petitions and prayers known unto God as stated in Philippians 4:6 (NKJV). Since our hearts are purified and there are no hindrances in the realm of the spirit, we can boldly approach the throne of Grace to obtain mercy and find grace to help in a time of need. But before we proceed, let's take a moment to clarify what grace is—and what it is not.

Grace is the Lord's unmerited favor; an expression of God's unfailing love for mankind. Grace is another undeserved gift from God, freely given to us despite our unworthiness. It's also an extension of God's mercy to us that we often abuse and take for granted. Grace allows us to approach the Lord free of guilt, unashamed, and fully transparent before Him. Because of this, we can approach the throne of Grace with the confidence that God hears us and will answer us according to His divine will for our lives. John 14:14 (NKJV) reminds us that, *"If you ask anything in my Name, I will do it."*

Grace restores our right standing with God and empowers us to fulfill the roles we've been called to such as fatherhood, motherhood, sisterhood, brotherhood, husband, wife, daughter, son, apostle, prophet, pastor, teacher, evangelist, etc.

Grace allows us to live in joy, experience peace in the midst of chaos, and endure all that life throws our way. Grace allows us to rise above it all and trust in our savior, Jesus Christ, during the process. According to Romans 5:20-21 (NKJV), *"God's law was given so that all people could see how sinful they were. But as people sinned more and more, God's wonderful grace became more abundant. So just as sin ruled over all people and brought them to death, now God's wonderful grace rules instead, giving us right standing with God and resulting in eternal life through Jesus Christ our Lord."*

Grace is not meant to be misused or abused by thinking "God knows my heart," or seeing grace as a *"SIN FREE"* pass. Grace has been exploited in the world as a pardoning system that absolves us from the consequences of our sins.

WHILE GRACE COVERS US, IT DOES NOT SHIELD US FROM THE CONSEQUENCES OF OUR ACTIONS.

I love how the New Living Translation states in Galatians 6:7-8, *"Don't be misled—you cannot mock the justice of God. You will always harvest what you plant. Those who live only to satisfy their own sinful nature will harvest decay and death from that sinful nature."*

Imagine how you would feel if someone repeatedly took advantage of your generosity. Now, consider how God feels when we abuse the gift of grace. Grace is extended to all, but it should not be viewed as a 'get-out-of-jail-free card.' It should be used to give every believer a sense of joy and comfort, knowing that we have a Savior who understands we were born into sin and shaped in iniquity. He also understands that sin produces anger, brokenness, bitterness, deceit, mean-spirited attitudes, manipulative ways, pride, selfishness, self-centered thoughts, unfaithfulness and so much more. Only by the *GRACE* of *GOD* did He look upon us and see His chosen people, His royal priesthood, and what He called and created us to be. That's the Grace of God.

The grace of God is so profound that it leaves the ninety-nine to seek out the one lost sheep. The Grace of God allows us to go through the fire and guarantees us to come out as pure gold. The Grace of God gives us a way of escape. The Grace of God humbles us before He allows satan to kill us. The grace of God makes bold declarations over our lives, as affirmed in Romans 8:31-39 (NKJV):

"What then shall we say to these things? If God is for us, who can be against us? He who did not spare His own Son, but delivered Him up for us all, how shall He not with Him also freely give us all things? Who shall bring a charge against God's elect? It is God who justifies. Who is he who condemns? It is Christ who died, and furthermore is also risen, who is even at the right hand of God, who also makes intercession for us. Who shall separate us from the love of Christ? Shall tribulation, or distress, or persecution, or famine, or nakedness, or peril, or sword? As it is written: 'For Your sake, we

are killed all day long; We are accounted as sheep for the slaughter.' Yet in all these things we are more than conquerors through Him who loved us. For I am persuaded that neither death nor life, nor angels nor principalities nor powers, nor things present nor things to come, nor height nor depth, nor any other created thing, shall be able to separate us from the love of God which is in Christ Jesus our Lord."

Know that God's grace is sufficient for us all, holding everything we need to live a 'submitted to God' life well. We serve a God that is the same yesterday, today, and forevermore. So, as we go before the Lord in prayer let us call upon our **Abba Father**, who withholds no good thing from His children. Let us evoke the **Just Judge** who will rule righteously on our behalf. Let us call upon our **Righteous King** who is issuing decrees in the realm of the Spirit. Decrees that say, "The enemy MUST RELEASE all that belongs to the righteous (immediately) because of our right standing with God." Everything that the devil has stolen from us must be released and returned to us sevenfold. According to Proverbs 6:31 (NLT), *"But if he (the thief) is caught, he must pay back seven times what he stole, even if he has to sell everything in his house."*

Just as Esther found favor with the king, who issued a decree to save the Jews, God will issue decrees on our behalf as it pertains to what concerns us personally and collectively as a nation. We must go forth in great boldness and with the authority that has been given to us according to Luke 10:19 (NKJV): *"Behold, I give you the authority to trample on serpents and scorpions, and over all the power of the enemy, and nothing shall by any means hurt you."* Recompense is coming to every believer who applies these scriptures correctly in prayer, as the Lord declares in Joel 2:25-26 (NKJV): *"So I will restore to you the years that the swarming locust has eaten, the crawling locust, the consuming locust, and the chewing locust. My great army which I sent among you. You shall eat in plenty and be satisfied, and praise the name of the Lord your God, who has dealt wondrously with you; And My people shall never be put to shame."*

Come! Let us go before the throne of Grace to obtain mercy and find grace for help in the time of need. Let us make our prayers and petitions known to GOD and stand in agreement, according to his word in Matthew 18:19 (NKJV): *"Again I say to you that if two of you agree on earth concerning anything that they ask, it will be done for them by My Father in heaven."*

According to John 16:23-24 (NKJV) *"And in that day you will ask Me nothing. Most assuredly, I say to you, whatever you ask the Father in My name He will give you. Until now you have asked nothing in My name. Ask, and you will receive, that your joy may be full".*

We stand on God's word and declare, as Ephesians 3:20 (NKJV) affirms: *"Now to Him who is able to do exceedingly abundantly above all that we ask or think, according to the power that works in us."* Lord remember us, just as you allowed the King to remember Esther and granted her petitions.

Take a moment to write out your petitions to God. Don't hold anything back and allow Holy Spirit to lead you during this time to ensure that it's in divine alignment with the will of God for your life. Petition God in your business, career, for your children, family, finances, friendships, health, marriage, ministry, relationships, promotions, and any other area you're led in.

Since we have confessed our sins and made our requests known to God, we can expect to see tangible evidence of His word, as stated in James 5:16: (NKJV) *"Confess your trespasses to one another, and pray for one another, that you may be healed. The effective, fervent prayer of a righteous man avails much."*

As we close this chapter, expect God to move powerfully on your behalf in everything you've prayed for. As an act of faith, do something that will try God at His word and watch God move on the seed planted in faith concerning your situation. May God bless you and prove His word to you. I declare that we will see immediate results from the fruit of our prayers, in Jesus' name and by God's grace and mercy that has been extended to us! AMEN!

WHAT OTHERS ARE SAYING

On February 8, 2024, God showed up mightily in response to our team's prayer. For months, the enemy had been trying to rob me, and significant funds had mysteriously gone missing—money that God had given me specific instructions about, which I had obeyed. I searched for those funds for months, but nothing turned up.

Then, during one of our team prayer calls, my dear friend Nadia prayed for me, using the strategies from The Blueprint: A Guide to Answered Prayers. She prayed with great detail and declared specifically that I would find the lost money before the day was over. Nadia began to war in the spirit, demanding that the enemy release what he had stolen. We stood on Proverbs 6:31: "Yet if he is caught, he must pay sevenfold, though it costs him all the wealth of his house."

Almost immediately after Nadia's prayer—within hours—the missing money was found! God delivered just as He had promised. And as if that wasn't enough, my glasses, which had been missing for two days, were also recovered immediately after our prayer—both items appeared before the day ended, just as she had petitioned God for.

My personal testimony is proof that God is still answering prayers. He is revealing His power as a sign that He hears us and loves us deeply! This blueprint has inspired me and my team to keep praying with strategy, to keep declaring the Word of the Lord, and to give the devil no rest until he releases all that belongs to us!

CHAPTER 6
BLUEPRINT AT A GLANCE

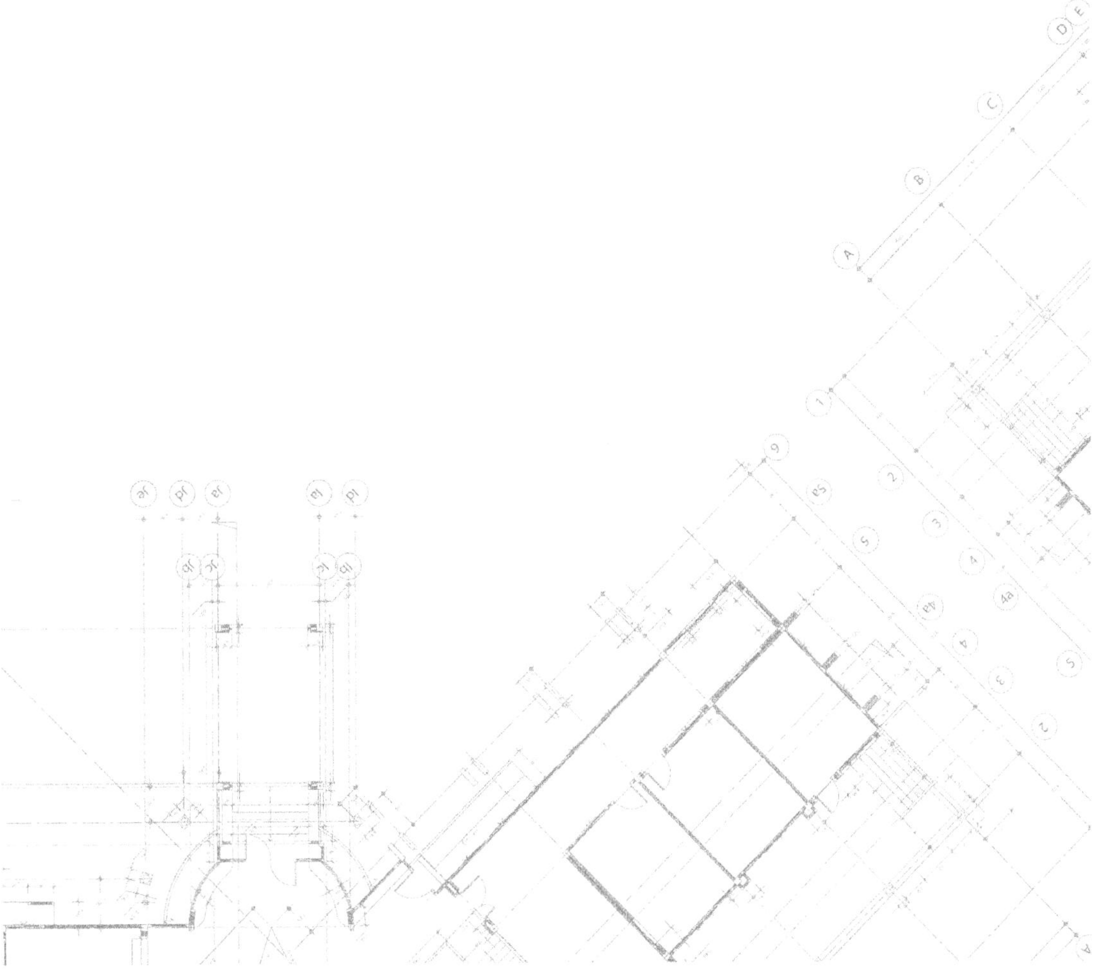

Since you accepted Christ as your Lord and personal savior, your God-ordained birthright has been activated. This birthright grants you access to approach God in prayer, believing that He hears you and will answer according to His will. I pray this book has been, and will continue to be, a blessing to the millions who choose to believe in God and stand on His Word. *"For we know that God is not a man that He should lie, nor the son of man that He should repent. Has He said, and will He not do? Or has He spoken, and will He not make it good?'* — Numbers 23:19 (NKJV)

Review this quick step-by-step recap of strategies for answered prayers, before inviting Holy Spirit to guide you in prayer..

Step 1: Approach God with thanksgiving.

As Psalms 100:4 (MSG) says, *"Enter into His courts with the password Thank you."*

Begin thanking God for His goodness and for being a Father who withholds no good thing from His children. Thank God for all that He is, recognizing His character and faithfulness. Begin to call Him by name, remind Him of how wonderful He is, and remind Him how much you need His guidance and counsel. Remind God of His everlasting kindness that He has shown toward you. Take as much time as you need to thank God in this moment.

Step 2: Confess and Repent

Now that you've entered God's courts, you are in a time of confession and repentance. Remember, if we confess our sins, God is faithful and just to forgive us and cleanse us from all unrighteousness. Allow Holy Spirit to guide you in this step and be sure to empty yourself before God. Repent for faithlessness, poor stewardship of money, people, and the ideas He's entrusted to you, disobedience, slothfulness, a lying tongue, pride, haughtiness, and lack of belief. Take time to be led by Holy Spirit and dig deep, especially as you repent for issues in your bloodline, marriage, or family that need healing and restoration. Take full responsibility and accountability for your role in these matters.

As Acts 3:19 (NKJV) says, *"Repent therefore and be converted, that your sins may be blotted out, so that times of refreshing may come from the presence of the Lord."* Take as much time as you need to genuinely repent before God.

Step 3: Pray for Mercy

Now that you have repented, it is time to ask God for His mercy. God's mercy overrules any judgment from satan. Remind God that His mercies never cease and are new every morning, as written in Lamentations 3:22-23 (NLT). As Romans 9:15-16 (NLT) says, *"For God said to Moses, 'I will show mercy to anyone I choose, and I will show compassion to anyone I choose.' So, it is God who decides to show mercy. We can neither choose it nor work for it."*

As you grow in understanding of God's mercy, I pray that He will begin to move on your behalf because you have humbled yourself and asked for His mercy.

Step 4: Approach the Throne of Grace

Now that you have asked for God's mercy, it's time to go to war for your bloodline, career, children, destiny, education, family, finances, health, marriage, ministry, promotions, and relationships. This is a time for warfare prayer, where you contend for everything that belongs to you and all that God has promised concerning you and your family. Position yourself in prayer as the mighty warrior you are, for though we walk in the flesh, we do not war according to the flesh. As scripture says, *"For though we walk in the flesh, we do not war after the flesh: (for the weapons of our warfare are not carnal, but mighty through God to the pulling down of strong holds.)"* 2 Corinthians 10:3-5 (KJV).

It wasn't until I read Rev. James E. Solomon's *Deliverance from Demonic Covenants and Curses* that I fully understood how satan legally operates against us, even after we have accepted Christ. Until we open our mouths and break agreement with the demonic covenants we've made with satan—whether formed through ancestral lines or personal sin—he retains the legal right to execute judgment against us. This is the time to destroy satan's altars. Call upon the God who answers by fire to consume every accusation against you. Burn up every demonic altar with your name, your family's name, your business, destiny, finances, health, marriage, and promotions on it, in Jesus' Name, AMEN! Flow in this vein and allow Holy Spirit to guide you in this warfare against satan's altars and accusations.

By the power and authority granted to me by God, I tear down every demonic wall and break off every chain of stagnation that has held you in place. I declare that every demonic cycle is broken, and every voice speaking against your progress is silenced by the blood of Jesus. We send public notice and issue a cease and desist in the realm of the Spirit, bringing an end to every judgment against you, as Colossians 2:14-15 (NET) says: *"He has destroyed what was against us…nailing it to the cross. Disarming the rulers and authorities, He made a public disgrace of them, triumphing over them by the cross."*

Now, come against every limitation blocking your progress. Break the spirits of delay, fear, and procrastination off of your life and family. Be sensitive to Holy Spirit, and allow Him to lead you into deliverance, breaking chains that have held you bound for days, months and years. I declare that this is your set time of freedom, for as 2 Corinthians 3:17 (NKJV) says, *"Where the Spirit of the Lord is, there is liberty."*

Step 5: Make Bold Asks

Now is the time to boldly ask God for what you desire, trusting that it will be done according to His will. After making your requests, start thanking God for what He's already done and what He is working on, as He perfects everything that concerns you. As Psalms 138:8 (NKJV) says, *"The Lord will perfect that which concerns me; Your mercy, O Lord, endures forever; Do not forsake the works of Your hands."*

As you walk in the freedom that comes from obedience to God, you will experience joy, love, peace, renewal, and refreshing, to name a few. Study God's word and find scriptures that speak to your situation. Pray God's word back to Him as a reminder of His promises concerning your life. This is an assurance for all believers, as Isaiah 62:7 (NKJV) declares, *"And give Him no rest till He establishes And till He makes Jerusalem a praise in the earth."*

Try replacing "Jerusalem" with your own name: "And give Him no rest till He establishes and makes 'NADIA' a praise in the earth." Be persistent, like the widow who continually went before the unjust judge seeking justice, just as we seek God's justice and mercy against our adversary. In Luke 18, the Bible tells the story of a judge who didn't fear God or respect man, but he granted justice to the widow just to stop her from pestering him. If the unjust judge granted the widow's request, how much more will our Lord do for us? As the Lord said, ***"Shall God not avenge His own elect who cry out day and night to Him, though He bears long with them? I tell you that He will avenge them speedily. Nevertheless, when the Son of Man comes, will He really find faith on the earth?"*** Luke 18:4-8 NKJV

Remember:

- He is our Abba Father who withholds no good thing from His children.
- He is the God who fights for us.
- He is a Just Judge who will rule your case with great compassion, favor, and mercy.
- The blood of Jesus is your Counsel of Defense, and it speaks better things than any accusation brought before God by the devil.
- Ask God to remember you as He remembered Hannah.
- Ask God to favor you as He favored Ruth and Mary.
- He is the same God yesterday, today, and forevermore.
- His blessings are met with a resounding YES AND AMEN.

God, as a sign that You have heard Your servant's cry, show us tangible evidence instantly. Remember us today, Lord. Let our situation be remembered. May these prayers rise before You like a sweet fragrance. Let the favor of God that rests on us go before us and move on our behalf today. In Jesus' name, Amen.

To the only living, true, and wise God—the God who cannot fail, who has no equal and no rival, who leads with an outstretched hand, who is a strong tower where the righteous can run and find safety; to the God who is a very present help in the time of trouble—thank You for coming to see about us. We stand on Your Word in Jeremiah 29:11 (NIV): ***"For I know the plans I have for you,' declares the Lord, 'plans to prosper you and not to harm you, plans to give you hope and a future. Then you will call*** *on me and come and pray to me, and I will listen to you. You will seek me and find me when you seek me with all your heart."*

As we close out "The Blueprint: A Guide to Answered Prayers," remember God's formula for kingdom success:

Acceptance + Thanksgiving + Repentance + Mercy + Going to the Throne of Grace + Thanksgiving =

- God's Authority
- God's Boldness
- God's Correction
- God's Divine Alignment
- God's Divine Protection
- God's Freedom
- God's Joy
- God's Happiness
- God's Love
- God's Lordship
- God's Peace
- God's Promises Fulfilled
- God's Provision
- God's Purpose Fulfilled
- God's Strength
- God's Sustenance

Scriptural References:

The Holy Bible is filled with scriptures that support this step-by-step guide, helping you gain access to God by simply entering His gates with the password "Thank you." In His sovereignty, God has provided us with a life manual that we must follow in order to live a "Submitted to God" life well.

www.ingramcontent.com/pod-product-compliance
Lightning Source LLC
Chambersburg PA
CBHW081341090426
42737CB00017B/3245